Fear Of Spiders

The Ultimate Guide To Overcome Arachnophobia Or Spider Phobia

James Scott

Table of Contents

Introduction

I want to thank you and congratulate you for purchasing the book, *"Fear of Spiders: The Ultimate Guide to Overcome Arachnophobia or Spider Phobia"*.

This book contains proven steps and strategies on how to conquer your fear of spiders.

Identifying the exact root of a problem is the best way to find solutions and eventually solve it. The same applies to a person who suffers from a specific type of phobia. That person needs to figure out the root of his phobia; Arachnophobia for instance. And that is what this book is all about.

Thanks again for purchasing this book, I hope you enjoy it!

Chapter 1: Cultural Origins of Arachnophobia

Biologists view spiders normally as creatures that are doing a great job in contributing to the maintenance of the equilibrium of our ecosystem. But these creatures being feared at or considered as evil contradicts their supposed helping role in our world. In other words, spiders are supposed to be one of the good guys. But throughout the history, their good guy image has been warped at some point. How did this happen? When did all these negative impression towards these creatures started?

People from different parts of the world have their personal stories to share, both good and bad, about their encounters with spiders. The outset of the fear of spiders can be traced back as early as the Middle Ages in Europe where it was believed to be the source of various diseases – contaminating food and water.

Furthermore, a spider's bite is believed to be poisonous according to Europeans which eventually led to illnesses and apparent death cases although the actual source of most illnesses and deaths during that time were rodents and fleas. This particular event was called the Bubonic Plague. Psychiatrists called the European's response misplaced fear since the spiders were not actually the real culprit of the said pandemic. But people still feared them despite the announced truth. And these unprecedented events definitely contributed to the development and spread of the fear of spiders in the European continent.

On a different account, prehistoric women had horrifying experiences with snakes, spiders, and other harmful animals which is believed to be the reason why most Arachnophobics are women. Ancestral women back then were pictured as naturally good child protectors making them more sensitive and defensive to anything that could possibly bring harm to them and to their children, while men are seen as the more aggressive and adventurous ones. They are believed to be hunters who are always out in the wild.

Other people in the ancient times, especially those coming from the Greco-Roman background, consider spiders as evil creatures as taught in the Greek mythology. Furthermore, spiders are given frightening attributes in the United States and the United Kingdom especially in horror films and children's stories. One example is the 1990 horror/comedy film by Frank Marshall entitled Arachnophobia. The movie received good reviews and acceptance from the market. One part of J.K. Rowling's Harry Potter also had a huge spider playing the role of a giant Acromantula known to be eating humans. This is one of the reasons why a huge percentage of Arachnophobics are found in these countries. Spiders appear as tough villains or monsters in movies, killing people and dominating most of the time.

On the other hand, some people still buy the idea that spiders are great contributors to the balance of our ecosystem. Countries such as Thailand, Papua New Guinea, Cambodia, and Venezuela treat spiders as normal human food and eat them. Fried spiders, for example, are considered a regional delicacy in Cambodia. Goliath bird-eater tarantula which grows as big as the size of a dinner plate is made a Tarantula Kebab in Venezuela. There are no apparent reasons how exactly people from these countries find delight in eating spiders especially in Cambodia though studies suggest that it must have started as a desperate response to the shortage of food supply in the country at some point. Others would simply say that it tastes good.

Moreover, recent studies about the nature of spiders were able to find alarming facts about the creepy eight-legged creature. Particular species of spiders are found to be venomous. Bites from majority of the species identified resulted mostly to allergic reactions or swelling of bitten areas. Worst cases led to excessive sweating, nervousness and nausea although recorded cases of spider bites leading to death were very rare for a very long period of time. These facts are probably the primary reason why most people fear spiders.

Looking deeply at the preceding statements, one can then assume that the individual perceptions about spiders, combined with the views of other individuals coming from different cultures, are the greatest contributing factors to the development of Arachnophobia across the continents. Through the years, frightening myths and exaggerated narratives about people's unpleasant encounters with spiders rippled to neighboring towns and eventually countries, forming this particular dominating fear of the fuzzy eight-legged creature called Arachnophobia. It's almost like a psychological pandemic devouring anyone who succumbs to its overwhelming smoke of intimidation. The frightening tales of spider encounters that echoes from the past and from random parts of the world caused fear and discomfort to anyone who hears it.

Chapter 2: Understanding Arachnophobia

The former things mentioned provide fundamental ideas about the personal acquisition and development of Arachnophobia. But the question is how exactly is Arachnophobia triggered?

Phobia and fear are totally different things. Fear is a rational response towards something that causes serious harm to a person. Majority of psychologists would define phobia as an unusual fear of a particular thing or situation that results to a feeling of anxiety and the need to immediately get rid of the stimulus or the object of fear. In phobias, most of the time, the fear is irrational since the object of fear is not that frightening at all in reality and people who doesn't understand it will find the fearful reaction of the person totally unnecessary.

In the case of Arachnophobia, spiders or other Arachnids such as scorpions, ticks or harvestmen provokes the feeling of panic and anxiety in an Arachnophobic – a person who is diagnosed with Arachnophobia. As mentioned earlier, a vast quantity of individuals all over the world is identified as Arachnophobics. In other words, Arachnophobia is named as one of the most common phobias known to people around the globe. This may sound surprising but who would indeed want to come in contact with a creepy fuzzy eight-legged creature or the likes of it? Though some people treat spiders as their pet and consider an encounter with one as good luck, a greater number of individuals still look at spiders as unpleasant and evil creatures due to cultural influences as mentioned in the previous chapter.

So Where Does Arachnophobia Come From?

Major researches have been made and various theories have been formulated to determine the exact onset of the development of phobias. But, the exact origin of phobias is still being figured out up to date. However, a person's fear of a particular object must always be coming from something. Most likely, phobias are acquired through a person's traumatic experience in a particular place or situation or with a certain object in the past. For instance, shared frightening stories from one person's encounter with a snake can trigger another person's fear of snakes. Or, a person who is afraid of being in a very crowded place must have experienced being robbed or stabbed in the past thus resulting to his acquisition of Ochlophobia – the fear of large crowds. Another person must have experienced falling badly from a tree that he broke his leg and resolved not to climb a tree again or go to high places where he might fall, which developed into a fear of heights or Acrophobia. Regardless of the kind of phobia, it probably came from something – perhaps, an ugly experience. The experience was so unwanted and traumatic, impacting the life of the person deeply that the memory have become almost unforgettable.

Likewise, Arachnophobia must have come from a person's horrifying experience with spiders or similar creatures in the past that he carried along as he grew up. The traumatic experience lingers in the mind and is recalled as soon as the person comes across a similar object or situation again. The feeling, sound, and emotion during that particular experience in the past come to a repeat causing the person to react instinctively. That person must have recalled the pain that he felt from the spider's bite or the unpleasant feeling of having a spider crawling on his neck or the fuzzy and gross looks of the creature that gives him the tingling and agonizing feeling. Regardless of what particular reason it might be, when repeated or recalled upon every encounter with the object of fear. The feeling of aversion builds up over time and is registered in the mind resulting to an increasing amount of fear and anxiety towards the object. The person's reaction in every succeeding encounter with the object will probably get worse.

The notions that Arachnophobia is genetic or innate have not been proven as a fact yet though there are study results showing women to be having more innate Arachnophobic tendencies compared to men recalling that our female ancestors are more sensitive to impending dangers than men. Some people picked up their traumatic experience with spiders as early as childhood. Though they were unconscious of their reactions back then, somehow the fear is awakened upon having a similar encounter with the object in the latter stage of that person's life.

Having said all these, the influence of the environment where a person lives contributes a lot to his being an Arachnophobic. For example, a child has been given the idea that spiders bite, and once they did it will cause apparent death to humans. This notion remains in the child's mind as he grows up and will have a high level of caution when dealing with spiders. As bad experiences with spiders are added along his life, the more fear and caution in dealing with spiders is developed in that person until he resolves to stay away from spiders no matter what. Afterwards, the person will show irrational responses during accidental encounters with spiders. The more horrifying encounters, the more the fear builds up eventually become a psychological disorder that is very hard to deal with.

Thus, the effect of Arachnophobia in a person's life will be a big problem if not addressed properly or dealt with during the early stage of its development. Others could just ignore it and say it's normal. But sooner or later they will realize that it's already interfering in their life.

Chapter 3: Symptoms of Arachnophobia

The severity of a person's Arachnophobia varies. Not all Arachnophobics show the same response upon spotting a spider. Some reacts irrationally just by hearing some people talking about spiders while others will not show signs of anxiety unless they saw the actual object that triggers their phobia. The levels of an Arachnophobics response towards the stimulus can be determined through Systematic Desensitization which will be discussed on the following chapters.

However, arachnophobics are very easy to identify. Generally, Arachnophobics can't withstand the presence of a spider or even just seeing a cobweb inside a room that they would run out of the room immediately or go to a different spot inside the house where there is no presence of a spider or traces of it. Others would scream and sometimes with matching shivering upon spotting a spider. Extreme Arachnophobics find it hard to kill spiders that they would rather choose to run away from it or ask somebody else to deal with it immediately. Sometimes, even just the thought of spiders or other arachnids make an Arachnophobic uneasy or a picture of a spider would cause them to panic. Arachnophobics will avoid any activities that might include any possible encounter with spiders such as trekking or hiking, camping, going inside abandoned houses, or going to the zoo. People who don't have any idea about their situation might find Arachnophobics ridiculous and would sometimes make fun of them which will definitely not help. Even toy spiders can bring a lot of trouble to a person with Arachnophobia.

On a different note, the Psychiatric Department of the University of Toronto labeled two different types of Arachnophobics. The first one is called a monitor who, by any possible means, searches spiders in any possible location like rooms, closets, the garage or cabinets and monitors its activities as soon as he finds one. Monitors can tolerate the presence of spider in one particular location as long as they don't come into contact with it.

The second type is called a blunter who is the exact opposite of a monitor. Blunters will do every necessary effort to stay away from spiders. They are the ones who, in worst cases, scream to death with all the exaggerated shivering and panicking upon seeing spiders. Hence, it is safe to say that persons with Arachnophobia mostly fall on the latter category.

Chapter 4: When to Treat Arachnophobia

Not all Arachnophobics necessarily need treatment. Some can still manage to live normally despite being an Arachnophobic. Although Arachnophobics are aware of their reaction during an encounter with a spider, they find it hard to control themselves most of the time. These people realize that they had to face the humiliating consequences of their reaction every time they come across the same situation and it's hard to deal with it. This is just one of the reasons why Arachnophobia needs to be cured unless he is willing to face all the challenges that he might face in the future.

A bunch of articles about an Arachnophobic's confession can be easily accessed on the internet. Most of them would say lots of funny stories about them being bullied or made fun at by insensitive peers because they are afraid of spiders. They would openly express in words how much they hate spiders and describe in detail their reactions on those traumatic experiences with spiders in the past. However, the common denominator of most articles will be about how these people feel so bad and sad about their condition and see themselves as dysfunctional members of the community. In other words, individuals suffering from extreme Arachnophobia might probably lack self-confidence.

So at what point should an Arachnophobic finally resolve to seek treatment for Arachnophobia? Psychiatrists would say that phobias don't necessarily need to be treated unless it already greatly affects a person's normal way of living. Phobias need to be treated when it already causes sleepless nights, diminishing physical and psychological health condition, disintegrating social relationship, or development of unhealthy personal behaviors.

Some people severely suffers from a specific phobia that the disorder prevents them from achieving their highest potential. For instance, a military trainee could be so overwhelmed by his fear of heights that he apparently failed the training or student was unable to recite his reading assignment in front of the class because of stage fright. More practical stories can be imagined where phobias are involved, interfering in the lives of individuals. When a phobia intrudes the life of a person to the point, then that specific phobia must be dealt with immediately.

Chapter 5: Overcoming Arachnophobia

Since fear is all in the mind as most people would say, who can better fix any human cognitive or behavioral disorders than psychologists? Arachnophobia can definitely be treated like other known phobias. Over the years, psychologists have developed a variety of ways to treat specific phobias like Arachnophobia. One of the most commonly used methods of treatment is the Cognitive-Behavioral Therapy (CBT) which will be discussed shortly. Others made good use of our rapidly advancing technology.

But before subjecting themselves to any method of treatment, it is very important that Arachnophobics made the decision to be cured willingly and not forced by anyone. The personal drive towards overcoming this specific fear plays a vital role in the treatment process. In fact, this is the primary step towards overcoming Arachnophobia. The second thing that an Arachnophobic must do is to choose the plan of treatment that he thinks he can do.

The following are some of the known methods and practical ways used to help Arachnophobics overcome their fear of spiders.

The effectiveness of these methods has been affirmed by majority of psychiatrists all over the world over the years.

Medication

Although medication is not what psychiatrists would recommend to treat phobias because of its temporal effect and possible side effects such as headaches, sleeping problems, nausea, or upset stomach, most people would resort to it rather than subject themselves to any form of therapies. Antidepressants, beta-blockers, and tranquilizers are some of the medication that is recommended to combat anxiety. Others choose to take medications probably because the therapy might be too much for them and they are simply not ready for it yet.

Systematic Desensitization

One effective method under Cognitive-Behavioral Treatment is the Systematic Desensitization which was developed by an African Psychologist named Joseph Wolpe back in 1950's. Systematic Desensitization is also called Progressive Exposure that works in three developing stages.

On the first stage, the object that provokes the client's anxiety is identified, let's say a spider if the client has Arachnophobia. The levels of anxiety vary based on the client's exposure to the object so an anxiety stimulus hierarchy is created during this stage. For instance, the client's anxiety level upon seeing a printed image of a spider might be lower than seeing an actual one. Shivering of muscles or sweating may occur as soon as an actual spider is placed near the client which did not manifest when just a picture of a spider was shown. The client's reactions toward the different representations of the object in each level will be the basis of the anxiety stimulus hierarchy.

On the second stage, the client is taught of relaxation techniques upon encountering the object. Some techniques that are being taught to the client are meditation and muscle relaxation. The third stage is the crucial one because the client must now try to apply the relaxation techniques that he learned while being gradually exposed to the object. The third stage might start with the client seeing a picture of the object, then seeing the object nearby to the point of actually touching the object and so on. The ultimate goal is for the client to gradually overcome the feeling of anxiety and fear in each level. Sometimes, the process is repeated until the fear of the object is finally overcome by the client.

Cognitive Reframing

Another method under Cognitive - Behavioral Therapy that is somewhat similar to Systematic Desensitization is called Cognitive Reframing. As the name of the method suggests, it's all about converting one's negative mindset about a particular object or situation into a positive one. Psychologists don't limit the use of this method only to persons with phobia. In fact, Cognitive Reframing is most commonly used by people who know the process to combat stressful experiences.

In the case of having an Arachnophobia, a cognitive distortion happens when an Arachnophobic encounters a spider. Normally, the person will either panic or freeze; breathing starts to become heavy and so on. Cognitive Reframing helps the person counter his fears by diverting his attention to other things that will overwhelm the dominating feeling of anxiety during that specific moment. Unlike Systematic-Behavioral Therapy, Cognitive Reframing technically does not have stages of processing the fear. The choice is weather to give in to fear or face it boldly and counter it. Thus, Cognitive Reframing requires a strong concentrating ability.

Hypnotherapy

This may sound weird but hypnotherapy was also affirmed by psychiatrists to be another effective option to treat Arachnophobia. One has to find a good professional hypnotherapist to be successful. Other psychiatrists would give an advice to combine hypnotherapy with other methods of treatment such as Cognitive Reframing and Systematic Desensitization for better results.

Virtual Reality

One of the more developed methods of treatment used to cure phobias involve the use of a higher level of technology such as Virtual Reality. The use of Virtual Reality technology especially in military trainings and curing cognitive disorders did not start until the 21st Century and it is constantly being developed up to date. Psychiatrists resort to Virtual Reality method if the client can't withstand or is not yet ready for the physical encounter with the object of fear during the therapy. For instance, Arachnophobic clients undergo a Virtual Reality simulation where they encounter spiders though virtually but provoke the same kind of physical and cognitive reactions as they would have with the real one. Psychiatrists still sees the effectiveness of the Virtual Reality method of treatment not far from the traditional methods. The Virtual Reality method is also used for other phobias especially clients with Acrophobia or the fear of heights primarily since it is much safer.

Smart Phone Applications

Just recently, an application to cure Arachnophobia has been released in the market designed for smartphone users. The application was a result of a partnership between a group of psychiatrists and a software developer. Following the Cognitive Behavioral Therapy model, clients get to play a game that requires interaction with a cartoon tarantula that gradually transforms into a more realistic image of a spider as the game progresses. The application is a prototype and psychiatrists are looking forward to developing a better and more convenient and accessible therapeutic solutions to phobias such as Arachnophobia using the modern technology.

Chapter 6: Further Steps

Despite the availability of these helpful methods in overcoming Arachnophobia, some Arachnophobics just don't have the right amount of courage and will to take a step forward and deal with their greatest fear. Spiders will always be cohabitating with humans whether we like it or not. And we can't deny the fact that these creatures can still harm us in some ways though at least in not so lethal ways. The following suggested actions can be applied by both Archophobics and non-Achrophobics for a problem-free cohabitation with spiders.

Education

Not all spiders are harmful to humans. Not all spiders that are venomous can bring serious harm. It will help to educate ourselves about the different species of spiders, their behavioral tendencies and identify which ones should be avoided and which ones are harmless. In this way, irrational reactions upon spotting a spider will not be necessary especially when it is identified to be harmless at all. A lot of informative articles about the dangerous and harmless spiders are available in the internet. Remember that they also take part in the balance of our ecosystem. Spontaneously killing a harmless spider is quite a bit harsh of a gesture.

Regular Cleaning

Infestation of spiders in a particular location could mean either food is abundant in there or spiders find the untouched, dusty, and cold area as their natural habitat. Modifying or regularly cleaning those particular places where spiders dwell or could possibly dwell is one of the best solutions to the problem. Another effective solution is to rearrange how things are arranged once in a while at home or a particular spot in a house where spiders might like to dwell. Changing the arrangement of structures in places where spiders dwell will cause them to move out instinctively as they feel vulnerable and threatened.

Most spiders found in houses like to live in holes or any untouched corners of the house on their web. The garage is also one of their favorite spots, dwelling on piles of random stuff junked in that cold dusty room. For some reasons, spiders are good at finding untouched or unmoved stuff to live in or lay their eggs.

Avoidance

Though cases of death due to a spider bite are very rare, it is always wise to keep one's self from danger. Places where a probable encounter with spiders could take place should be avoided as much as possible. Educating one's self about the nature of spiders will help a lot in this action such as knowing the natural habitat of spiders found outdoors and indoors. Others coming across an unpredicted encounter with a spider would just shoo it away by using a stick or doing random hand movements that will intimidate the spider.

Conclusion

Thank you again for purchasing this book!

I hope this book was able to help you to overcome your fear of spiders.

Finally, if you enjoyed this book, then I'd like to ask you for a favor, would you be kind enough to leave a review for this book on Amazon? It'd be greatly appreciated!

Thank you and good luck!

Made in the USA
San Bernardino, CA
07 February 2018